Tethers a Collection

I0142361

Tethers
a Collection

Joli M.

Copyright © 2019 Joli M.

All Rights Reserved. No part of this work may be reproduced or transmitted in any form by any means without express permission from the author.

Cover Art by Joleene Naylor

This title is available in e-book formats at participating retailers.

Contents

Acknowledgements...3

Preface...3

Part One...4

Part Two..15

Part Three..20

Part Four...26

Part Five...37

Bibliography..46

Acknowledgements

A special thanks to Deborah Marinelli and Jennifer Quail. Your encouragement and love for the written word inspires me. A huge thanks to the writers I have met over the course of my journey. Without your support this book would not have been possible. I thank God, for seeing me through to this moment, and beyond.

Connect with me:

Instagram: @Jo_M_Schu
Facebook: Joli Schumaker
Email: Jo.M.Schumaker@gmail.com

Preface

There are few things in life more exciting than seeing your creations go out into the world. I think this goes for artists of every medium, scholars and scientists included. I bring Tethers into the wider world with a mixture of disbelief and anticipation. Collected, they showcase my personal trials in both the inner and outer worlds. Observations and doubts that few have been privy to, up until now. They also display my heart, and my complicated relationship with courage, loss, strength and love. It is a snapshot of my life, expressed through the lens of my first and most native language-Poetry. Thus, the mixed emotions. As you enter this space, it's only natural that I give context to the title of these writings as a whole. A tether is a tool used to ground, bind or keep something steady. It can also be used to leash or cut short things, thoughts or the steps we take. Neither use is exclusive, but both are relevant in our lives. Though the forms they take can differ. This is a look at my lifes' Tethers.

Part One

The Space

Happy-a word
A
Thing
I Watch
Pass
As a
Parade
Of skeletons
A term I've scrapped-once and again, and drop
At entry ways to rooms above my
Roofs line; where boxes
Lie
As entombed borders
To the thoughts, I've put away
Some hints
Of photo'd
Faces
Poking out-lit dim
By hall light
And late-night Moon's call
Through branches and
Dust
Too ancient to clean, from rouge fingers
And wide eyes even those
With best
Borne intention-their words
Too
Soft
For this space; where
I've
Buried the failure and pain; not
All mine
With some borrowed from the dead
And those
Still living with their ghosts
Like charms
Lined in silver

And swung loose on
Copper chains-framed
Like trophies
Of a life, not at that
Time, to be tamed
To live in one
Life's line-the process on repeat
Till what remains-are solely
Boxes
In a space, I
Cannot keep

Shine

We shine glass figures
Framed in sunlight
And fire-clear portraits
Of
What
We've seen
Veins colored
In the shades
Of
Moments, that have come
And gone-like broken steps
We take
Toward
Futures, ill-defined and
Slippery like stones
Beneath
Rushing creeks-matted
In moss that
Clings; and
Forces
Our feet
On
New
Paths
We shine, built
With

Sand bars
And memories; that burn
Our cracking
Fingers, and
Bruised
Toes

With Sugar on Top

Pretty
Please
With
Sugar on
Top
Pretty please, all fingers
Crossed
Pretty
Please, with toes curled tight
Pretty
Please
Just
Stay
Tonight; dreams that float
Me
Full
Of helium and fire like
An
Air
Balloon
And pull me higher
Until
The sun comes-peeking through
With its slim
Sharp rays
In
To the mended tears of my air-balloon patch
Work; where
I've
Sewn
And

Re-sewn, all my hopes
With the
Hands
Of a child, lacking machine
To hold my stitches
Tight, against airs' currents-as my night
Shifts
Back to
Day and
Candles
Scurry
Back to sleeping, leaving
Only a grey, misty
Trail to betray their once, unsleeping
Presence
In the black
Of long nights
At
The carpet, and the hoping page
Black dripping
From the wick
Like an air-balloon's smoked
Remains
Touching ground
As a giant
Without shape
To portray
What once
Might
Have
Been

A Lion's Paw

I remember-his paws. Big and Bright, like
Cedar wood, always stood-then
Each claw, and nail
Defined
Deep grooves
Without outstretched fingernails-that

Must have been fierce, once
That must have been sharp-once. Like a shark's tooth-the kind
Hung in gift shop
Windows; bought trophies of a war
I remember
His legs-slender and proud
Muscled like the arms beneath
Etched drawings
All in black
Weathered
And
Warm
I
Remember linoleum floors, beneath lions
Mane
And fan light wafting oven's heat
Unsteady

Unbidden Sweet

Nostalgia
Rears its' ugly head, as I witness
Waves
On water
And sun in grass
Light war-flashback
To the good
The bad
And the wonderful-to the darkness
That
Sometime
Crept below door frames
The way
A ghost must
If blocked
Free entry
Nostalgia
Shows in faces I'd forgotten in
Photographs
Places I'd left

Behind me like pebbles
On a beach-front, spilling
Through
Fingers widespread
Nostalgia hits me
As I go through paper
Words
Wide and uneven
Spilling
Down the page
Like water
Over
Rocks in some, strange wood
Nostalgia comes
An unbidden friend; dosing poison and sweetness
In equal measure

Elephant post

Pack me
Away in a box with
Peanuts
And paper. The
Deep lines of
Styrofoam-teasing elephants; flooding-this
Room-so full
I cannot
Breathe. pack
Me away in plastic
Envelopes
No window-to watch through
Pad the space
With
Bubbled paper; and cardboard string
Till the words stop. Too muffled
To
Make out, among
Swift silence-the reprieve
So temporary
At least-in

The two, to three
Business days outside
Of weekend
Hours
When the
Silence ceases to breed
Or
Care
For tease-of peanuts
In a wrapping
Without crunch

Coast-Shack

I
Dream
Of California
Like a far-off
Place
With sun and sand, the flashes
That
Snatch-my imagination
I
Dream of Boston-streets cobbled
And
Colored swirled
Hate, existing, in the
Decline
I dream of wandering-to my
Hearts' boundless
Content-to taste
Sand
And sandwiches-born
By
Coat-side
Shack

The Summer

The summer, we caught an

11

Eel-on the fishing line
At Park side
Water
There was blood on fingers
And an odd, ugly face
Peering out; unblinking
Eyes steel
And grey like wordless
Strength
Was in effect, a silent will
And a fierceness
That fish don't seem to know
Always
Looking shocked
As they're lifted, flailing or
Still in fear
From the water's slim
Protections
And looking
Ever
More terrified, if
They again
Meet
Water's surface rushing
Down
Like Would-be victims
Of a hound's
Hunt
But lacking
Feet to run, or holes
To hide
In; where none can touch
Their scaled, shimmering
Backs
Or thin, strong tails
That feel
Like oiled leather
On my hands
Crusted
Hard

By the bone beneath

To the Picture

Ode
To crumpled sidewalks
Up
Rooted by tree; trunks bent over
Backwards, and covered
With weeds
Growing unchained to expected
Form; moving
As quiet shade
From
The eye's whirling storm
Ode to
Airborne chalk
Dust
Swept up quickly in a breath
And ode to the pictures
Held tight
Inside my breast

Bubble, Creek

It's funny
But
The words are gone
Dissipated like silent film
In reel, is
Stocked. But the colors
And the
Touch
Of calloused hands
Remain
The days-are
Colored
Standing
Terracotta
Snaps
Of mosaic, in motion
It's

Funny
But the
Sound
Is gone
Save
The breeze; and
His smile-and bubbling
Creek
Water

Indefinite Whirlwinds

These stories-I tell myself
Are long. They
Have a start; one quick beginning
Floating to me
From
High, distant
Whirlwinds; tinged
In colors soft
And mute
Of character
With middles strangely crafted
And half-drawn
Ends broken by my
Strange ideal, that all
Must end
In song
And
So, the song of monsters' hands
Leaving
Prints on windows, in
The moonlight; and of mirrored worlds
Where I exist
In repeat, and of far places,
Where
Red dust
Is kicking in the wind
Continue
Indefinitely

Part Two

Fire

Tuck me
Into your heart
Pocket me safely
From
Storms
Their wild intent banging quick
At our hollow doorways
And glassless
Windows
Long
Free of
Moth munched curtains; lying
Shriveled
In a branchless
Tree
Soaked in poisons
From the cellar
That we
Keep
Bathed in dust and
Grime
From the memories
We should cherish
And the feelings
We should keep. The faces
We should
Remember, with our
Failing
Eyes and flitting
Hearts, that live
Like moths
To flame, when the smell
Of old carpet
And sweet-smelling wood
Rot
Come back
To us-breaking

Through the sunny day
Like an ancient reaper
Seeking soil
To bury
His hands
Beside

Three Strikes

Three strikes; till bell starts
Again. Three strikes
Till time strays
From stillness-and the air
Moves
Rushing
Past
My shivering
Frame; drenched in
A
Cold
I
Cannot shake
Three
Strikes; till my lungs
Start
Fast
Three strikes till goblins
End
Where
The room-will shift
Right
Back, with the stairs
In places
I can
Reach-with my toes
Not my eyes, when glancing
Up at polished glass plates
Glittering
Stray light
To corners, and layers

Innumerable
Three
Strikes, till time
Moves
Onward. Away from what was
Real Once
Before the clock
Struck
Three

Valley of the Shadow

I broke away from arms
holding warmth
Unworthy
The comfort-I felt in unified
Breath
I Broke
And
Ran
From the blaring sun
Tripping
Mirror to my shadow
Mute
I did this
Crossing low
Dry
Spells
Of earth
And Canyon cracks
Large
Almost Crevices
I could
Hide
Between 'Till the
Sun, standing high
Finally
Lays down low
And again, at dusk
I Start

My Journey
This-is my Valley
My source of shadow
And dusk's love. The dust
At my feet
Sparkling
Sunlit
Gold and regret. Flash-frozen
Tears stupefied
By sun
This is my valet
My valley of shadows
The canyon
Of
Flash
Frozen things, littered
As peaches on sand and scattered
Wide
Like
Crab apple's
Stems

Part Three

The Letter to My Shadow

Hello to you
My shadow, who stalks my steps
With warped reply, as I pass
Beneath
A streetlight lit
With glowing
Bulb whose gaze is harsh
Even cold
As it forces to the forefront of this muddied
Mind, every seasons' regret
Lying
Pushed
And pulled further along,
Down the rabid
Hole
Of a rabbit mind,
Frenzied and fevered
With "What if's?" and "I could have's..."
Hello to you the clumsy
Being
Who shrinks beneath sidewalk curbs
And dances on the grass
Of half-
Browned
Lawns, while mowers whistle tunes
Like cheerful saws kicking up
The green
Hairs
Till all
Is thick-piled moss trimming
Braided-metal fences
I know
You'll jump
If I
Lend you one
Careless hop
Pulling legs, just in

Front or behind
Your antics; so
Much like
Fun house
Mirror shapes, pull
Me
Back
Through
Time, to when I could
Escape
Into the mystery
Of your changing
And be quite
Content
Back to
A time
Where regrets
Had not
Almost poisoned me, to you

Lion of Steel

The words come
Thrashing tongues
With fire
And flight
Fear
of
The
Stand, with sound's beacon attached
Accounted, by the stranger eyes
That take Hollow sounds and
Make them whole. Sweet and thin
Like
Candy
The words come stacking
Tongues, that
Leave a taste bitter, and sweet
New and old
Sounds fury, softened-like a lamb's
Wool

Coat. Sound's scars forgotten-like
A
Lion-of steel, and start that trips
At
One First
Light

Seeking Life at Sea

I wished
And I
Wished
For magic
For a cure to a family's curse
Set by witches or poor circumstance
Years or decades, passing us slow
After it's hurtful and purposeful
Casting
But it seems-through trying
Trials
And trails with dead ends attached
That branches
Have died roots
Have dried
Puddles have dealt their
Short reprieve
And
There's really no saving
What
Has
Passed
Should
I set out
To sea?
For
A cure
Ask the fated three
If they know well what comes?
Should I pray on my knees
With tears in my eyes; asking for healing
From all things that

Demise-the tree and the stump
The roots
And
its' dying branches
Or
Should
I set cast out to
Sea, with all the good things
And take in water, aware of the leaks
Patching
As I go. Flow in blue waters
Breathe In my sails
Drink in
The wind that
Comes
Flying forward
To the islands
Where trees are borne strong
And given
Good
Names
And rain that splashes in branches above. For drink
And for
Life

Ocean's Eyes

Reluctant
Daze sighs into life
The things, and parts I
Cherish-yet abhor
While little
Hands
Wash yellow, orange red
Rocks
In long
Stream that bubbles cold
Reluctant, heavier
Sighs
Follow closer too like a shadow that won't let go

Can't release
For fear
Of falling over; then down
Down, down
Away, and far
From
View. Never to be seen in
Light
Reluctant eyes, with their
Reluctant sighs watch
Each ripple
Of
Each wave follow course, and swiftly
Die
Identifying too
Close
With the wave that leaves the beach in tears
Soaking only the edges with its' grief
Well spun, and
Run
Washing the miles
Beneath
With salt, and shells and life

Part Four

Sand

Dead
Somehow
The word is a final crack
Of hammer to wood
Gone
Somehow the word
Is a quiet thing that vanishes
A whisper in
The wind
Lost
A word somehow
Inviting empty sentiments
Read hollow
Like the hole
She left
In room dark, curtains
Drawn tight. Cold is the heart
Beats
Trail, scrubbed clean of evidence
Warm
And cool are
The tears that streak
From faces
Drawn ashen
And
Sketched in layers
of Sand

Lace Bared

I'll bear it
These feelings strung
Like Christmas lights, on
Skin-near tattooed
For
How they weather those
Things which watch

And
Wait
For weakness to show, through
The glare
Of lights, that color skin
In all their hues
Of consequence
Almost armor
To a mind
That's without sense
Of when
To stop
Or start displays
Or even how
To change the colors back
Once
I have seen
The darker hues
I hide
Inside the bright; almost
Targets
For the aims
Of
Play
Almost Breakable
As silver bulbs
Gleaming pieces
Lying
Carpet bound
With New year's
crunched confetti
And ashes
From the fireplace
Well feed

Clutching fingers

We
Are
Born inconvenient

With one breath, draw our screaming lungs to life
Raise
Our
Screams up high, demanding Mother's
Touch; while she lay, breath half
Caught up to her own
Raised wines of pain and hoping
Pushes; that brought us out all naked
And shivering into the fluorescent beam
That plays at first sun for our clutching
Curled fists
Eyes squinting
We
Remain, and inconvenient
To our Mothers' tries at conversations
With adults who seem
To linger, with long boring subjects we don't care
For
With a clutch at a pant leg
And pantyhose, fingers messed in grease
And paired with long
Fingernails we want cut
We are an inconvenience
Yet as we grow
We step
Out of Mothers'
Shadow
Find our fingers pulling clothes
And pushing on the panty
Hose, finding ourselves
In
An empty
Room
Staring down the mirror, where
Our Mother's
Face, peers back. Reflecting what
We wish we knew
Just prior
To
The curtains

Black
We are
Born
And inconvenient
We came, intruders in the night
To the lives of
Two who were enough
Forever changing their
Minds about the 'cuteness,' of a spit-up
Bib
Handed down from great Aunt Marge
Recycled
From
A
Cousin's child
Twenty years back before the end
Of textiles
And for nine months
Building hype-as the belly grows
Only to emerge, a whiner
Only to
Emerge a crier, held together with tape
And band aids'
Noses running
Full
Of
Jokes that make us
Laugh
So hard we pee
And eventually forgetting why we laughed
Moving past the silly to
The serious
From the Band-Aid's to the stronger
Stitches
That keep our hearts
Thin
Strung together in vague
Shapes
That once had 'human,' clear spoke on
A

Placard
That once
Had
Innocence inscribed
And we
Remain an
Inconvenience
They can't say our names
Or keep our
Faces in mind, for the terror they feel
At our change. They reflect
At
Their mirrors, and
Blame themselves for the brokenness
Remaining inconvenient, we
Cause them pain so deep
Unspeakable
Love so insurmountable
That they can't leave
Behind the spit-up
Bibs, and Band-Aids
And they'd trade
Every moment lost
To fix
You. We are born
Inconvenient with inevitable
Heartbreak riding in
Our clutching, greasy fingers
An inconvenience
Untradeable
Unforgettable and forever
Adored
Full of whining, full of found
Hope
That cycles on as expected
As
The day

Of the Things

A
Touch of sadness; rings
In a new year
Where summers
Have changed. No more simple
No more set
A
Flit of regret
Hangs
In the
Air. The
Way that
Smoke lingers on the line between
Days
There
Lies
A
Touch a
Taste of sadness
Tinging air
Heavy
And
Lungs
Full of the things
I should
Have known
Would
End

Mortal

Could
I speak it
Into life
This feeling that precedes
A
Falling house
Of
Precious
Set cards

Edges Keeping
One
Another in their
Place
At
This time
Only air
Between them
As they stay. Withstanding sounds and trembles
Of
Old, burnt-out
Quakes that used
To
Bother me the way that
Curled
Linoleum seeks to
As it rises
To topple
My
Feet; to steal
My steady steps
When I
Should take them
Could
I
Speak them? Into living words
These sounds
That play through
Me like mute violins
Heard
Through peepholes? Or
Should
I
Speak them? Are they secrets
For
The masses to keep
Hidden
In plain sight on mantles
With old
School Photos

And
Wry smiles proudly
Immortalized

The stutter of the fireworks

The spitting
Pop
Of bombs, bursting smoke and colors
Keep stark
Against the blackish
Blue
Until they dwindle
To the next
Bursting over
Faded
Smoke
Layered messy
All upturned colors
From Half empty cans
Of wistful
Purchased
Paints once meant to color
Walls or
Encourage
And Delight
A
Little set of
Eyes and tripping feet
That
Kick their
Shoes off
In doorways
Muddied
By last night's rain
And todays heavy thunder
At this deafening stutter, we ride
The
Thoughts
Across the blackened

Blue
Until they vanish
Wiped
Behind the cloak of well-meaning stars
Taking fire's
Dusting
And shaking
Itself clean
A weightless cloth
Until
All is still
And stale
Just strange
Enough
To leave one
Last
Impression

Battle

Another game begins
Jump-starting
Battlefields
Play. Toy soldiers in the grass
All stood
At attention, set to scatter
And tag
The enemy's back
With colors
That eyes should not see
In daylight
Where all
Is innocent
And intentions always
Sweet. Souls searching
For
Good
Without qualm
And our battles
In daylight a try
At worlds' word drinking   35

Though wet
And
Worn with sand
Written long
On wrinkled paper

To Dry

Hung to dry
My sheets embroidered
With a thousand things
I should
Have
Said. Hung to
Dry
My
Shirts, that border
Between my eyes, and
Things
I've
Said. Hung to
Dry, these things I
Hoarder
Hung to dry
These words
I Keep

Part Five

Handmade

I
Don't
Want to fear
The days unfolding
Like flowers
That await my hand
Petals breaking
From stiff
Green
Bulbs
Their light
I thought long spent
I don't
Want to fear the soil
Where my feet
Have planted
Their hopes
And dreams thin and
Veiling fantasies awakening
My eyes to
Beautiful storms
Backlit
With silk so dark, and smooth
So riddled
With light
That the frame is magic
I don't want to Fear
That which
Stains my soul with pictures
Of stillness and
Glass paintings that reflect
Their filtered colors. Through clouds
When they
Come
And do
Pinch me 'awake,'
To my place I

'Should' be
Though I'm grounded
Elsewhere
I don't want to fear
The things that grow
In other gardens
To feel
I should step from
My
Soil
To the bed
Of dyed, thin
Flowers. The soil entrenched
In tumbleweed
Nests
Better off for birds of prey
To tear
And feed
To car bumpers
On dry highways
I
Will
Keep my future close
And breathing, drinking
Storms for breakfast
Imprinting still beauties of the aftermath
That may come
As filtered colors
Through handmade windows
Of which I know
Some have
None

Something Borrowed

I Know your lies
Your life behind
The curtains
A masquerade of mirrors
Reflecting pleasant words

Like 'See you soon,' and 'Love true,'
I
Know your tremors
In
Tailored ands or
Buts
Playing notes
To
Please. And those hurricanes
Trapped just
Behind
A placid grin
You keep locked
Up as bedtime scares
And
Shadows I know
Them
Like the ache in my joints before a storm
I know them
As the strain in my
Calf
The burn
On my arm
I know them
Being
Something
Borrowed

Where time Stands

The paved paths
Cry: their crumpled sides
A Tribute
To time
And the weighty footsteps
He brings. Almost monstrous
To eyes who knew
These roads as home
And safety nets
From
Darker

Things
But time, he comes
No
Mal
Intent
No wicked wishes, no triumph
Sent
In that
wild, forward gaze
That sees time passing
Oh so
Differently
This time
He comes
To
Do
The bidding
Of a clock that runs
A known world, chiming
Minutes
And hours somehow silently
Till we're lulled into a sense
Of the inevitable
Change. Our bodies
Speaking softly
Of the coming
Of
Another age
Attempting soft warning that
Today's words
Belong
Only to today, and the ears
That listen
Close
To them
As time is
Striding slowly behind our
Steps like shadows
Pressing
Into sidewalks

And the grass of hills
Neglected mowing
Pressing fences
Into mud and bringing
Flood. Like cleansing
Rivers
Come to wash this strip
Of caked, cracking layers
That
Were footsteps in shoes
One moment
Small
And grown as the water
Comes
Called by the Quakes
Of those same timed steps
Following behind us
Like wishful
Old men
Out for summer's
Stroll with
A head full
Of memories of the way
Things
Used
To be

Warm Reflections

I escape
Your warmth, wriggling
Out
Like a child
from blankets meant
To wrap my skin
In plush
I escape your hopeful gaze
As I don't share it
I see
Darkness in my midst. I see

My
Sins
Hanging like curtains black or
Grey
But I smile at your
Light
Out of habit, out of need
Let the Grin
Out
Still
Suppressing its composure
As I hide my
Heart in shame
These are
Words
I cannot say
When my lips are there
In
Time. Things I can't express
Until
Darkest
Day
Looms over the fullness
Of
The mind
I keep
And so
I escape your
Warmth. Myself then the pain
Of reflection
That
Keeps
Me running
And so,
I escape your warmth
To avoid a fight
To avoid the mirrors trimming
And the scaffold
Near my soul
To keep my heart from

Prodding
Its own
Scars, and stitches
The Bruises
Galore
And I know
Running is not
Enough
To leave behind skies
And then perfect
Words
To leave behind dreaming's
And shapes
In the clouds
The loneliness
Of dark streets and Ice-cream caked
Toes
The warmth of a kitchen
With a dripping faucet
In the daylight
I know
That running
Is not Enough
Yet I run
From your words
And your arms
And
These things
That have stayed
Painted to my palms, in
Warmest colors

Season Change

Up from Soil
We Rise and sink
With
Each
Seasons' end

Then search out
Our
Fires in the sun
Till
Ill-got
Clouds
Keep barred our way
From clear sail skies
As sunset flies, stronger
Then we knew
And grant us light
To
Continue
For a season
Change

Afterthoughts

I was raised in Upstate New York, where I learned to love intermittent rain and aging buildings. My new home in Northern California is far sunnier, with new homes and businesses cropping up every day. This new home inspired me to write about the old. This is how Tethers came to be. I hope these Poems have made you laugh, cry and reflect on your own lives. This is after all, what Poetry is meant to do. Good luck and God bless, as your seasons change.

Bibliography:

"Tethers" A Collection of Poetry

"Echoed Wishes"

"A Voice in the Downpour"

Visit Smashwords.com/profile/view/Jolimarie for more on my latest projects. E-book versions of these titles available at most online retailers.

www.ingramcontent.com/pod-product-compliance
Lightning Source LLC
LaVergne TN
LVHW041209080426
835508LV00008B/878